Raw

DEDICATION

To the people who have given me everything, my parents.

To be all born blank,

empty and honest,

We were all born raw

ACKNOWLEDGMENTS

Everyone who has played a role in inspiring one of these poems, I would like to thank you. You surviving your struggle is reason for someone else to make it through their own.

RAW

SMOKE SIGNALS

Thick air and clogged freedom,
Deploy search parties to Ukraine,
and Syria and Egypt. Iraq called.
They said they want their bombs back.

Libya sent a "Get well soon" card
We haven't heard from God yet.

But the Catholics, they're praying
The Jewish, they're praying
The Muslims, they're praying

We enter the world
and leave the world
looking the same
oppression begins
where unification shatters

Supremacy is contagious through
Sex, scandal and slavery
Infamous slums, scums and secrecy
Listen- cries of the voiceless
Begging "Save me... save me.. save me"

Suffocation shoves a knee between our legs
Pins down our arms, yanking our hair

It steals breath
When we try to say
You do not own me

I'll gag choking on liberation

America bleeds white, not red
Meaning the yarmulke is patriotic
Meaning the hijab does not strangle a person
The way white America slips a noose around necks
Tying a knotted bow with ropes of discrimination

The country I would die for is killing me
My death cannot speak for me

If you think being a man
is measured by the beer you drink
the car you drive
and how hard you throw a punch
You are not listening

If you tell me I am too smart
to be black, too peaceful to be brown
too pale to be sober, too fat to be beautiful,
too ambitious to be a woman
You cannot be listening

Allah Hu Akbar is not a curse, it is a blessing
Colored skin is not inferior, it is human

White America, bite your tongue.
Nothing of yours is sacred
In your graveyards
Villains lay next to freedom fighters
Lost bodies slain together
R.I.P that's resting in pain

We will peel off our skin
Pale, bronze and black
Fold it into the barrels of your guns
So in your civil wars fighting for freedom
Erupts our sacrificed independence

In the smoke from our ashes
We Rise Again,
you hear whispering

We are worth more than where we came from.

WALLFLOWERS

When we were younger,
we were taught to keep our hands to ourselves
we were taught to grow up and make a change
but we never learned
when was the right time for which
we never learned
when it was better to bite our tongues
and hold back punches in an argument
or when to hold someone's hand
to pull them off the ground
we never learned that loving someone
shouldn't mean changing them
by molding them in our palms
to make them smaller
so they could fit in our fists
because some people
can get so small

it's like they've disappeared
even when they're still there.

PLACEHOLDER

As a woman
I was born
half full and half empty.
and as a woman
my biggest mistake was
biting my tongue
and tasting the
blood of everyone
who has been there
before mine

ORCHESTRATED

I look at you and I see all the ways a soul can tear
and I wish I could reach inside you,
let my hands carve you like wood
To make strings that stretch you whole,
and hollow enough to finally hear

How beautiful your echo is even when
You're empty inside

I AM MY MOTHER'S DAUGHTER

You have seen the world in more ways than one.
It hasn't always been fair to you,
but you already know that.
The years have grown over your body like vines.
Stretches on your stomach from giving birth,
Wrinkles blanketing your eyes with worry.
You always worry.
In becoming my own person,
I've tried so hard to break free from you.
I always thought being independent meant being alone.
But I wonder how much of who I am is who you were.
And I wonder how much of who you are
is who I'll become

TOKENS

Pick someone who
knows you by the sound of your laugh
a look in your eyes
the way you say his name

pick someone who notices the little things
so that if you ever forget who you are
there's not a detail that's missing

ORGAN DONATION

The saddest thing I've ever done
is make someone else happy
is break my own heart
into tiny, little pieces
Just to fit better in their hands.

SCALES

When something bad happens
I lay in bed and rank my problems
You have survived worse, I'll think
You've been through things much harder than this
And then I realize
My worst is someone else's best
No matter how difficult I have it,
Someone else will have it harder
And while that does not
Make my problems any easier
It gives me a little more to appreciate
And the more I appreciate the little things
The more I learn to value everything else

THE OTHER WOMAN

If the world was black and white
you'd look at her and see color

and my body would be ash,
my bones would be chalk

KNOT

You hold my hand
like my veins are made of thread
like a single tug
could unravel me

USED

If you have hurt me
I will beg you to leave
I will beg you to go
So I can suck myself up
and spit myself out
to be chewed on again

ATTACHMENT

You measure our love
by telling me to leave

you didn't even notice
I'd already left

you didn't even notice
I was cringing
and cringing

you couldn't even let go.

MIRRORED

It's easier
to pretend you don't want more for yourself
When you're tired and hurt
and feel as if everything that could be done already has
feel as if the best you can be
is nothing more
than a reflection of someone else

SACRIFICE

To love without hurting
To give without taking
is all the women I know
knew how to do.

REGENERATION

Why do you hate dark skin
Dark is the color of soil
and soil births beauty
No matter how many times you cut a flower
it will always grow back

THE FIRST STEP

If you have woken up
and gotten out of bed
you have already done the hardest part
And the rest will be better

STRIPPED

This is it
this is all I have to give
if you take anything else
I won't be me anymore

HOW TO FORGIVE

Forgiveness is
taking the knife out your own back
and not using it
to hurt anyone else
no matter how
they hurt you

FOSSILIZED

And like everything else
in time it will get old
to decompose and disappear
and that's okay too
because sometimes the beauty in something
is that it won't last forever

BAD WEATHER

When it's cloudy outside
I'm reminded of why you left
I'm reminded of your yelling
louder than the thunder
shuddering through the rain

BAD MEAT

You skin my body
and are so confused
when shame guilt and regret
are all that live underneath
are all that have taken the place of love.

MIGRATING

Let it go
let it change
find your place within it
and if you can't
let it change again

STAY

When we fight,
I don't want to talk to you
but I don't want you to leave
and that's how I know
I've fallen in love

SHARING

Nothing belongs to you in this world
Everything is earned, given or temporary
The sooner you understand that
The happier you will be

THE DEVIL WEARS FIRE

Just because you mean everything you say
Does not mean other people do too
We live in a world
Where people light fires
To create something bigger than themselves
Just because they like the look of it
Just to see everything that can be swallowed
And just to watch others be destroyed

A BODY FULL OF GARDENS

When something is taken from you
Say thank you
Now there is space
For something else to grow

PILLOW TALK

We want to hold each other's bodies
But not each other's pain.

MY NAME IS NOT HANNAH

My parents moved to a country
Where I have to degrade
the pronunciation of my name
to fit in another color's mouth

LIVE FOR LOVE

Out of everything,
I think falling in love
is the most beautiful thing I've witnessed.
It's what anyone can surrender to,
it's the strongest passion I have ever seen.

People change, and not what they wear
or where they work-
people change their hearts.

Being in love will have them smiling,
calling their mothers after years,
baking muffins for no reason.
Giving money to the homeless,
getting a degree. Staying clean on a drug test.

Being in love can give someone a reason to live,
What could be more beautiful than that

ABOUT THE AUTHOR

Raised between two different cultures, Hana likes to learn as much about the world as she can. She uses writing as a medium to express feelings on the clashes, problems and struggles she sees around her. She has articles published in The Huffington Post as well as The Connecticut Post. She currently studies Biology and resides in Manhattan.

Made in the USA
Lexington, KY
05 March 2017